ZOOM: IDEA THAT SELLS EVEN IN ODD TIMES
PROVEN INCOME-BOOSTING LESSONS

BY

MIC L. HARRY

COPYRIGHT
Copyright © 2020 by
MIC. L HARRY

All Right Reserved. And No part of this book may be used or reproduced in any manner whatsoever without written permission except in the case of brief quotations embodied in critical articles or reviews.

Table of Contents
Introduction
Chapter One: Backgrounds are not Barrier
Chapter Two: Birth the Idea
Chapter Three: Idea incubating
Chapter Four: Tenacity of Purpose
Chapter Five: Learning Through with the Idea
Chapter Six: Unperturbed with "Nay Sayers"
Chapter Seven: Be Around Smart Go-Getters
Chapter Eight: Attitude Matters
Chapter Nine: Build Experience, Build the Idea
Chapter Ten: Competition is Never a Threat
Chapter Eleven: Communicate the Idea and its Essence
Chapter Twelve: Manage All Resources
Chapter Thirteen: Resting Not On Oasis
Chapter Fourteen: Give Rooms for Improvements
Chapter Fifteen: Touching the World with the Idea
Chapter Sixteen: Insufficient Funds Never a Threat
Chapter Seventeen: Strategies to be above Board
Chapter Eighteen: Your Home matters
Chapter Nineteen: Go Legal
Chapter Twenty: Sustainability: A Must
Chapter Twenty-one: Projection for Future

Introduction

The impressive story of Zoom as the go-to teleconferencing software is very much connected with the innovative vision and character of its CEO and founder, financed by famous Silicon Valley venture firms, who attained the holy grail of both a successful IPO and hyper-growth. By taking a tour back in the early days of when Eric Yuan was a student to the period when he founded his company, there are many lessons that today's entrepreneurs stand to benefit from. When rigorously applied, these lessons can be your guiding compass to manifest your vision of building a world-class company or successfully working in one.

Chapter One: Backgrounds are not Barrier

Like most first-generation billionaires in the United States and around the world, Eric Yuan, the CEO, and founder of Zoom Video Communications, is a self-made billionaire who worked his way up the ladder of greatness. He was born to parents who were mining engineers in the Tai'an province of Shandong, China, sometimes between 1969 or 1970. Even though he is Chinese by birth, he is a Chinese-American by ethnicity, and as fate will have it, he later went to the United States in 1997 to pursue his dream of being a teleconferencing engineer.

Eric Yuan schooled at Shandong University of Science and Technology, where he obtained a Bachelor's degree in Applied Mathematics and Computer Science. Afterward, he enrolled in China University of Mining and Technology, where he obtained a Master's degree in Geology Engineering. Subsequently, he went to Stanford University, where he underwent an Executive Program sometimes in 2006.

He married Sherry, his long-time sweetheart, and their love story was the architect of what the world witnessed as zoom. This great innovation of teleconferencing had a ripple effect on many sectors of the world because it made teleconferencing in every sector of the world easier and better. They got married sometime in 1992 and have since been blessed with three children. Very little is known about his wife and kids because Eric is somewhat discreet about his personal and family life. In fact, he refused to disclose his exact date of birth. What is known about his age is a clear estimation.

Early Life
Eric Yuan's entrepreneurial spirit has always been with him since childhood. When he was in 4th grade, he gathered metallic scraps and recycled them to make copper, which he sold out to interested buyers to make some profits. In his first year at the university, he discovered that his long trips to and fro to see his girlfriend was actually tiring, so he conceived an idea to create a video-telephony software that could help him communicate with his girlfriend from his screen even without going to actually see her. That was the beginning of the zoom idea. He eventually came to America to see to it that his idea became fruitful – and it eventually was.

Career

After Eric got his Master's from China University of Mining and Technology, he went to Japan, where he stayed for four months to run a training program. In 1995, Bill Gates spoke at a seminar in Japan, and it was from that speech that Eric Yuan found his inspiration. In 1997, he found his way into Silicon Valley to pursue a career in tech. Eric had to apply for the United States visa about nine times before he became successful in acquiring one. When he came to the U.S, he spoke very little English. He was lucky to be employed in a now-defunct teleconferencing start-up, WebEx, where he was among the lucky twenty people to be hired. Cisco Systems later bought WebEx in 2007, and Yuan was promptly made the vice president at Cisco Systems in the department of engineering because of immense contribution to WebEx. Yuan proposed a video conferencing system that is adaptable for smartphones at a Cisco management conference in 2011, but his idea was rejected. Since Eric conceived the idea, and only he understood its profitability. He later left Cisco Systems to consolidate on this idea, and this saw the birth of Zoom Video Communications.

Zoom went public in 2019 when its IPO (Initial Public Offerings) was made, and it was at that time that Eric Yuan attained the status of a billionaire. The novel coronavirus that caused the 2020 pandemic saw to it that his wealth increased because most businesses and school around the world shifted their activities online. Eric Yuan's net worth as of 1st Sept 2020 was valued to be US$16.4 billion, an amount that was more than three and half times higher than what he was worth at the start of the year.

Personal Life
Eric got married to Sherry, his long-time girlfriend, when he was 22, while still a master's student at China University of Mining and Technology in Beijing. They live in Santa Clara, California, together with three children. He became a citizen of America in 2007 and has been listed as one of the 100 Most Influential People of 2020 by Time Magazine.

Chapter Two: Birth the Idea

When Eric Yuan Birth the Idea of Zoom

The Zoom video conferencing application is now utilized as the desired teleconferencing alternative for everything from yoga classes to governmental meetings surged in the number of users it acquired during the coronavirus pandemic. As lockdown was imposed across the globe, zoom found its way into the vocabulary of most quarantined individuals, and the growth of its share has mirrored its massive growth in its global recognition. And its recognition has since doubled since the pandemic spread the world over.

Now fifty, Eric imagined the Zoom idea when he was a Master's student during the periods when he had to undergo a strenuous 10-hours journey by train to see his girlfriend, who he later got married to. Because of his tech-inclined nature, he thought to himself that there must be a way to talk with his sweetheart without having to meet her physically.

When he came to the United States in 1997, he began programming a web-conferencing software for WebEx. When WebEx was acquired ten years later by Cisco Systems, Yuan tried without success to convince the fat cats at Cisco Systems that the smartphone era demanded a more intuitive, simpler form of business and web video-conferencing, completely designed for the purpose of teleconferencing. His critical break away from Cisco Systems came in 2011, and from there, he went on to build his own company. Initially, there weren't many financiers queuing up to take stake their money because they all presumed that the video-conferencing industry was already saturated – but Eric borrowed funds from family and friends to finance his project. Eric's judgment was consistent with the turn of events. The coming of smartphones in the market created a gigantic demand for portable teleconferencing software, and zoom became the go-to option for many users.

Eric's Zoom application has made development in China, his home country, and a natural extension of Zoom's processes: about one-third of his company's staff are in China, and a large chunk of its development and research is outsourced there. But what once appeared to be a strength for the company has risked turning into a liability. Zoom's connection to China may be a loophole in the American markets that are becoming apprehensive of China's ambitions. For now, Eric, a beloved employer who lives by the watchword "hard work and stay humble," is generally known for his simple and happy approach to life. When he was queried about the first thing he'll do after the end of the pandemic, he said, "I'll give my workers a hug." But the wild ride of Zoom really may just be at its beginning phase.

Chapter Three: Idea Incubating

After Eric persuaded that someday he'd start a company, and impressed with the strides of pacesetters like Bill Gates, he set his sail down to the U.S to have his share of the tech boom. Eric joined WebEx when it was only two years old in the summer of 1997. Being an enthusiastic and young programmer cum entrepreneur, Eric will use most of his Friday nights to write codes and use his Saturdays for soccer games.

Leveraging on the dot-com bubble's high spirits and with teleconferencing programs becoming more enjoyable courtesy to increasing internet connectivity, Webex became a public company in July of 2000 and was subsequently bought in 2007 by Cisco Systems for a whopping $3.2 billion.

Shortly after, Cisco saddled Eric with the responsibility of leaning the engineering team of WebEx. But Yuan was still not happy. He was deeply convinced that the services WebEx was offering to its broad clientele were inadequate. Whenever a user logged into the platform, WebEx's computers will have to validate the product (Mac, PC, or Android) and which version of it should run. Eric was convinced that there are better ways to make things more efficient. When there are many people in the queue, the connection can be strained, resulting in choppy video and audio output. Modern technologies like mobile screen-sharing were absent on this platform.

Eric told one of the earliest financiers of the zoom project, Bill Tai, that, "Someday someone is going to build something on the cloud, and it's going to kill me." One year after unsuccessfully trying to persuade his boss to reshape WebEx's modus operandi, he gave up and went on to build his company. In his own words, Eric said, "Cisco was more focused on social networking, trying to make an enterprise Facebook," he says. "Cisco made a mistake. Three years after I left, they realized what I said was right."

For Eric, the biggest challenge was persuading his wife, so erroneously thought that Eric was about to make a big mistake by forgoing his employment with Cisco systems.

He told her that though the journey wouldn't be a smooth one, he may live to regret it someday if he does not take the action he intends taking.

Eric asked for the assistance of friends, family members, and investors to help him raise the sum of $250,000, which he intended to use to pay the 30 engineers who worked on his idea with him. They aimed to create an innovative solution for teleconferencing and decide on the application to build on top. Due to their immense trust for Eric, the financial backers, including a past CEO of WebEx, Subrah Iyar, financed his start-up venture (then known as Saasbee) with $3 million.

Zoom released its first consumer app in 2013 after creating a previous version of Eric's teleconferencing software and evaluating it with tech company customers across Silicon Valley. It started gaining popularity with business customers, with Zoom being used by more than 3,500 companies within the first five months of its release.

After two years, that number had risen exponentially to around 65,000 enterprises, leveraging Zoom's video conferencing tools with more than forty million people directly using the application. One of the reasons for this widespread adoption was that Zoom provided a free service that individuals could use to access video calls on their smartphones or synchronize in conference rooms with conventional conference equipment. Zoom still provides its basic services at absolutely no charge at all, but to enjoy extra features and encourage more users to use the app, corporate clients can opt for subscription services.

As a veteran software developer with several patents relating to real-time communication technology under his watch, Eric believed that the advent of tablets and smartphones introduced new possibilities that make mobile video teleconferencing more affordable and usable than before.

In 2011, Eric knew he would have to abandon the safety of his lucrative executive position to set out on his own venture if he wished to create a business the way he intended to do it. He left Cisco and started creating his own software framework for teleconferencing while seeking the financing he would need to create a product and start a nascent business.

His company expanded to recruit almost two thousand employees in less than a decade since he created Zoom, thus almost increasing its revenue by twofold by about $620 million as of 2019. In April of the same year, Zoom released its (IPO) initial public offering, an offering that became one of the year's most successful debuts. Zoom's stock has increased by more than twofold since the beginning of 2020 due to the rapid surge of consumers amid the COVID-19 pandemic, earning Zoom a market value of around $42 billion. (Some observers on Wall Street claimed last year that the Zoom's stock is overpriced relative to the revenue that the company generates). Eric owns about a 22 percent stake of Zoom and currently worth about $9 billion.

The teleconferencing industry was reasonably dense when established his San Jose-based Zoom. The industry was controlled by big tech companies like Skype, Google, and Cisco. That made it hard for Eric to persuade venture capital companies to fund his business idea, but he won the support of friends, family, and venture capitalists like Dan Scheinman, a former executive at Cisco Systems, who had faith in Eric's zoom project enough to hand him a check of $250,000. (Dan Scheinman is presently a member of the Zoom board, whose share in the venture after Zoom's IPO in April was valued at almost $176.5 million).

Much of Zoom's early growth was organic; its entire marketing strategy at that time relied on word of mouth promotion. They didn't even have a marketing team until 2015.

In some instances, Eric himself also dived into customer support by communicating directly via email to users thinking about canceling their subscriptions. He would respond to them when a user cancels in an attempt to know why they want to cancel. He gained a lot from this experience, and some of his consumers he communicated with also went towards becoming faithful, long-time consumers.

Chapter Four: Tenacity of Purpose

Everyone in business will always face competition from people offering similar services. It is normal and should not be discouraged.

You're not working hard enough, or you're disconnected from reality if you don't have competition. Cultivating the right degree of determination when you are faced with competition should earn you the trust of those you are trying to influence. That is one of Eric Yuan's secrets of success. Because of his company culture and work ethic, he is loved and respected by his employees.

Tenacity of purpose is a concept of resilience that is most relevant when it relates to influencing others in the workplace. Tenacity is the capacity to demonstrate loyalty to what you trust. To succeed, you should continue to pick yourself up, cleaning yourself off, and quickly getting back on your feet.

At its peak, tenacity helps you stay open to ideas because you'll want to continue to learn about what could make your business better. If you have tenacity, instead of outright dismissal of something to the contrary, you can look for ways to bring others towards your target, even if that means changing your path or some of the information along the way. You keep your intent true.

Tenacity of purpose should not be mistaken for being stubborn, bloody-minded, or pig-headed, neither of which can help create a working employee-employer relationship. Intransigence, unable to alter your ideals or consent to a superior ideal, is another word that clarifies that you have to stop and probably have a change of mind.

In a team, these behaviors can create conflict. In a Glassdoor review of how content the employees at Zoom Video Conferencing is with the company's leadership, it was noted that more than 95% of workers responded favorably. This can only be attributed to the leadership quality of Eric Yuan, and also the fact that he makes sure that his employees are provided with the best working conditions. Who doesn't like a free lunch? Now you catch the gist!

Chapter Five: Learning Through with the Idea

Your work culture starts with your hiring processes. Zoom assesses applicants on whether they agree the applicants will provide others with satisfaction and accept the quality of care. If they accept zoom's fundamental principles of care, they would be soul-motivated and work harder for their colleagues and their clients. Zoom will ask them when they interview applicants to tell them about a notable case wherein they showed concern for others.

Employ self-motivated people to work for you. The world of business is fast evolving, so all workers should be busy learning new things, new technology, and new capabilities. Teach your employees to encourage themselves to overcome obstacles and have the courage to carry on without depending on someone else to inspire them daily. One great advantage of teamwork is that everyone gets to learn from one another as they keep working together. Various researches have shown this over and over again.

The work culture of your business is the number one most significant things you need to accomplish. From there, almost everything will flow into place. The workers at Zoom have a philosophy and reputation for caring for others. Zoom expects its employees to be concerned with the community, the business, their colleagues, their clients, and of course, themselves. Zoom does not want its compassionate principle to be a one-off that is clarified and never addressed again in staff development, so it's displayed in every place on the walls of Zoom's lobby. And if humans get to every learn anything that sticks in their mind, it is by repeated exposure to that information they want to learn. To this end, repetition is a very effective means of making people learn. Eric has a firm understanding of this fact.

If your workers are not satisfied, all aspects of your business will be equally affected. One thing Eric's Zoom understands is the fact that they do not trivialize the happy moods of their employees. Zoom is so keen on this, and that is why there is a Zoom Chief Happiness Officer (who also doubles as a sales representative) who has a "Happy Squad" crew of her own. The crew consists of around 25 representatives inside Zoom who are in various job roles and places but who have offered to help deliver on driving culture. Zoom's Chief Happiness Officer partners with the happiness squad to schedule activities such as trips and volunteer days. As a business, Zoom acknowledges one worker per quarter who goes beyond and above to externally and internally create happiness.

The phase needs to be as pleasant as a result. Here's a classic example: while Eric was still with them, Webex went public, and they had a big party. Then, it was purchased by Cisco Systems after staying a decade with Webex, an incident that all the staff were excited about and lauded. According to Eric, he learned a vital lesson from these occurrences about outcome vs. process. For each of those deals, it took several years to achieve the outcome, and Eric felt that with both, everybody was just after the result. It was from these experiences that Eric realized that the process should be appreciated as passionately as a result, was appreciated. Irrespective of how great the endpoint turned out to be, if you don't love and learn the process, in fact, then coming to work every day will be one hell of a task to you and very demotivating. Eric understood from those periods the vitality of relishing the broad range of the process and of feeling the joy that it can bring.

Five Methods Eric Yuan Uses Empathy to Lead

1. **Take Employee Happiness Seriously**

This ideal is a daily routine in Zoom. For Eric, he makes sure that he personally assess the happiness of his employees by asking them about it. If his employees feel happy coming to the office, Eric will encourage them to do just that, and if for any reason they prefer working from home, then he'll; be happy granting their request. For Eric, all that matters is that the output is not lacking, and efficiency is in check. Also, there is no way you and your business will go to the next level that you desire if you don't plan to take your employees there.

2. **Be Transparent and Keep Communication Open**

When Eric was queried about how he ensures the happiness of those who buy from him, he made a wonderful note that earning their trust is the only way to make them happy. And that is why Eric made sure that every dealing between him and his clients is transparent and open. He also interestingly noted that every one of his customers is like extended family members to him, and with this mental disposition, it is not rocket science to see just how effective communication with customers will turn out to be.

3. **Give Heed to Your Flaws**

The Zoom team has been trained not to trivialize their customers. To them, negative reviews are more important than the positive ones because they directly communicate to them what areas they lack incompetence and the best method to apply when solving it. To anyone keen on personal development, it will be straightforward to see how consistent yourself can lead to becoming a super-efficient being. And that is exactly the testimony of Zoom.

4. **Work Smarter and not Harder**

Eric numerously admitted to the hearing of others how Zoom made his life better. He seldom travels and has dedicated a large part of his life to becoming happy and teaching people just how to be happy. This happiness disposition also fuels his ability to work smart and not just engage in a series of hard uninspiring work. There are Zoom teams in Europe, Austria, Kansas City, Japan, and of course, Chine making it absolutely efficient and easy to hold virtual meetings with their teams at other locations rather than having to travel.

5. **Go for People Who Care**

When he was asked about his fellow executives and board members concentrated on customers when most care about their numbers, Eric Yuan made it clear that he is tasked with going for executives and investors who interest his customers at heart. He does this by making sure that everything is transparent and open. In fact, this has gone on to become a part of their company culture. There must be an alignment between the employees and customers at Zoom and their investors. With his team, Eric is a firm believer in a vigorous life-work balance, and this ethic is visible in how they work.

Chapter Six: Unperturbed with "Nay Sayers"

The truth is that there will always be naysayers among us. Everyone who has attained great success in their lifetimes will tell you that these set of people will always lurk around the corner waiting for the perfect opportunity to strike. No success story is without them in lurking around somewhere in the picture.

Like most of his contemporaries seeking to go to the United States, Eric was also searching for greener pastures. Because of the tech boom in Silicon Valley at that time and the advent of the internet, Eric honestly believed that the country has a lot to offer him. After getting his visa applications rejected about eight times, giving up will be the most logical thing to do for most people. But not Eric, who has a firm determination to go to Silicon Valley and accomplish his dream of building a system that will make virtual face-to-face communication easy. After submitting the eighth application in a period that spans two years, he was accepted on his ninth trial.

Eric had one great limitation when he came to the United States. He spoke very little English, and it wasn't so easy getting a job in an English-speaking country. He later succeeded in beating the odds of not getting a job in Silicon Valley sometime in 1997, and WebEx absorbed him into their workforce.

While at WebEx, he performed excellently and was well-known by his colleagues. His hardworking nature saw to it that he quickly rose up the ladder of leadership at WebEx. Just when he was about to carve out his niche in WebEx, the company was acquired by Cisco Systems. He was promptly given the post of the vice president at the engineering department at Cisco Systems, and this important position made his job pivotal to the company's success. While at Cisco Systems, he initiated many patents and used his creativity and idea generation skill to develop fantastic solutions to numerous problems that Cisco Systems was facing then.

But while at Cisco, an idea struck Yuan. He knew the immense profitability that his idea of creating a portable teleconferencing software is, largely because of the increasing smartphone dominance in the market. He begged his superiors at Cisco to adopt his idea, but all his persuasion fell on deaf ears. Some of his colleagues criticized the idea and didn't make any positive comments about it. It took great persuasion before Eric persuaded some friends, family members, and investors to help him finance his Zoom project. Convinced that the market needed his idea, he later left the Cisco systems in 2011 to start his now-famous Zoom Video Teleconferencing. As of this moment, Zoom offers a trustworthy cloud platform for voice, video, chat, and content sharing runs across desktops, mobile devices, room systems, and telephones.

Eric's story has shown us that believing in oneself and not taking into account the negative things people say about us is one way to go far in life. It is okay to accept positive and constructive criticism and look for room to improve to become a better version of yourself. The truth is that you wouldn't always be right. For Eric, negative reviews from customers are his guiding compass to sail his company to a better destination. Always make room for change and learn when to adjust your initial plans to accommodate change, and you will be shocked to see how far your company will go with your company.

Chapter Seven: Be Around Smart Go-Getters

For most giants and captains of industries, choosing the right people to work with is non-negotiable. The right people creates an atmosphere that is favorable for the growth and success of any enterprise. As everyone conversant with the last century's event will carefully note, the people with ideas are the world's major shapers.

One great thing most employers are looking out for in their employees is the possession of a go-getter mindset and being smart enough to know when to harness an opportunity and how and when to deploy one. For Eric, working with the right team members is as important for your business's growth as having a large customer base. Nothing truly beats a team with the right mindset and insight on what to do and when to do it.

The right team for any establishment comprises smart go-getters who are keen on getting the job done. They are also leaders, and their enthusiasm is contagious, and it is what other team members need to propel them to success. The chances are that a company that does not have the right team will never attain its full potentials, and that chance is so big that it is almost always true.

Being A Go-Getters Can Be What You Need to Succeed, But How Do You Become One?

You may be asking yourself what is so special about go-getters—a lot. But the biggest question you are probably asking now is how to spot one. Well, some characteristics are common with go-getters that almost all of them do possess. Go-getters are people with healthy self-confidence; they are risk-takers, ambitious, hungry, and people with great communication skills.

Don't get it twisted. Being a go-getter is not all about adopting a personality type. For instance, there many industry giants, and first-generation billionaires are introverts. A classic example is Bill Gates. Eric Yuan is another example. All that matters is that you adopt the particular mental disposition that go-getters have, and becoming one will be sure. Go-getters are people who burst with energy and enthusiasm when doing their work.

Chapter Eight: Attitude Matters

Nothing Beats Attitude

Eric Yuan has his yardstick for measuring success. While speaking on stage to Connie Loizos from Tech Crunch, Yuan went ahead to disclose his discontentment with the M&A of WebEx, relating to it as if though it were a yesterday's event. According to Eric, this deal is bad from one when seen from an employee's perspective. But he submitted that nothing is wrong when it is seen from the perspective of a shareholder. He also related how embarrassed and dissatisfied he becomes whenever he spoke to a WebEx customer.

For over fourteen years that Eric spent on working on Zoom, he didn't record a single satisfied customer. This caused him great sadness, and even his engineers were not left out. In his own words, Eric said, "every day, it just felt like, oh my God, what happened?"

Right from when Eric Yuan started building his Zoom application and making a company out of it, he always stressed the importance of "making a happy customer" and "caring for their needs." He also highlighted that "culture" and "trust" are both important ingredients that'll ensure customer satisfaction and the company's growth. Also, when someone questioned him about a new investor at Zoom, Eric told him that he is happy to work with the investor because he believed the investor could 'make a friend for a lifetime." Even though these statements from Eric may look like something that has been rehearsed to be said during the shooting of a movie, there is reliable evidence that suggests that these were actually Eric's reality. According to the over 1,300 different employees who worked at Zoom, a Glassdoor review showed that most of these employees were happy working at the company. This is reflected in their 4.9-star rating of the company.

More than anything else, your attitude is what determines if your employees will stay or leave. If the CEO of Zoom has an attitude of not caring for his employees' well-being, it would have reflected in a number of ways. For instance, how efficient a company becomes is ultimately a result of the amount of work that the employees put in and how well they relate with one another and with their customers.

In fact, Eric was named Glassdoor's CEO of the year after he got a whopping 99% approval rating from his employees, beating Marc Benioff of DocuSign Daniel Springer and Salesforce and Jeff Weiner LinkedIn.

How did Eric Yuan's Ethic of Applying "Care" and "Happiness" Help in Zoom's Daily Operation?

- **Foster a Culture of Customer-First with the Happiness of Your Employees in Mind**

While reflecting on his days at WebEx, Eric Yuan firmly believes that Zoom's success is contingent on one fundamental principle – ensuring culture and environment that makes their customers feel secure and well catered for. Even though this may seem overly simplistic, Eric Yuan has staked all chips on this apparently simple concept. Zoom will have to compete against other similar brands in the market in terms of user experience and product satisfaction. This shows why their adopted company culture is very vital, and it really paid off in terms of employee retention and customer satisfaction.

When Eric was questioned about going into competition with Amazon, Yuan answered that he revered the company but had one issue with it. According to him, Amazon does not fashion its services and products to deliver happiness to enterprise customers and their employees. He ended the reply by saying that his company does not have to worry about Amazon.

- **Employ Based on Potential and Trust and Not on Former Big Company Achievement**

When Eric went on to build his company, forty-five engineers from WebEx came along with him. As the nascent company kept scaling, the hiring mode of Zoom became dependent on trust. To this end, Eric, the recruitment was largely dependent on internal referrals. Employed workers were tasked with recommending people to the recruitment selection board, and many got their employment letters as a result of this. About 65% of Zoom's new employees are still selected by this referral method even today.

- **Make Existing Customers Your Priority Before Thinking of Winning New Ones**

Zoom's success has placed the company on a pedestal where it will effectively take charge of the lead into the future with new features and insights. When Eric was asked the next priority of Zoom, he said that his relationship with his existing customers is his guide in decision making when dealing with the new ones. To him, maintaining the happiness of existing customers is more important than ensuring the happiness of the new ones.

Chapter Nine: Build Experience, Build the Idea

Industries are Driven by Ideas

Building an experience for any venture is a sure phase for any business idea. Most great inventions and enterprises are ideas that were carefully built and deployed. The late eighteenth century and the early nineteenth century was greeted with massive idea generation and deployment. During that period, we saw the industrial revolution that was spearheaded by the effective use of resources like coal to drive industries. The industrial revolution saw massive growth in virtually all segments of the economy. For instance, the transport sector was massively transformed because this oversaw the development of trains fueled by coal. As a result, railways were built in many parts of the world, and economies and governments grew massively.

Business moguls like Cornelius Vanderbilt maximized this revolution and carved an empire for himself. The next revolution that greeted many countries was when oil deposits were discovered and developed methods. John D. Rockefeller and other oil businessmen earned profitably from this, and they so do other businessmen. Economies grew further, and alternative use of the energy gotten from oil was discovered and also deployed. Gas plants were built, and new use of it was discovered. During this period, new heavy-duty vehicles and sophisticated military hardware like tanks who run other energy sources other than petroleum were also built.

The coming of the internet witnessed another revolution that many love to call the information age. At the click of a mouse and in a split second, information can be transmitted across thousands of miles. In fact, this discovery has led to more knowledge and research about outer space, and we now know that the sun, for instance, is no longer the center of the universe as was erroneously believed.

Information and Communication Technology

While it is true that virtually all segments of the world have considerably transformed in the last century, no sector has been massively hit with this transformation, like the information and communication technology sector. New models of laptops and smartphones are released with more sophistication and appealing features than the former every year.

In the telecom industry, it was this immense potential that Eric Yuan saw and built his company around it. When the company came to its full potential, it wasn't hard to see how immensely beneficial it turned out to be. Although this did not come without years of hard work and "incubating the idea."

Chapter Ten: Competition is Never a Threat

Competition is Your Best Bet

At Cisco Webex, Eric Yuan wasted a lot of time chatting and embarrassed with Webex clients because he did not see a single pleased customer. He knew that the client had to be satisfied. His approach was video first attitude when setting up Zoom, and the formula for success proves a lot for too little. Zoom is a success because its technologies and customer experience satisfy customers more than rivals, and they appreciate what the customer needs. During the tumultuous times, Zoom was productive because they did a lot earlier, and it's like they were planning for this. Zoom is a successful enterprise, and they have worked tirelessly to address major challenges, targeted at a dilemma that has plagued many individuals and centered on the consumer.

The tale of Zoom's prosperity and Skype's demise contrasts with how customers play a major role in a company's longevity and growth.

Skype first began in 2010 as the go-to teleconferencing application for about 40 percent of the population. However, below to its sluggish response to consumer feedback, this business struggled, particularly in a seamless user interface. It used peer-to-peer engineering when purchased by Microsoft, which is only successful on PCs but not on smartphones. It is evident that in their everyday lives, numerous individuals are now using their smartphones for teleconferencing. Microsoft was unaware, and even though Skype was continually improving, users say the staff was annoyed if a sudden upgrade broke their presentations.

Zoom did nearly all the things that Skype refused to pay heed to. It began in 2013 under the management of Eric Yuan, who was the previous Cisco VP of Engineering in Webex teleconferencing tool development. He decided to leave Cisco out of dissatisfaction from the executives on non - adherence to negative consumer reviews on Webex. Some of them were challenging installation approaches, a lag duet to slow internet connectivity, and audio problems. Yuan's confidence in the first concept of a consumer made him the kind of CEO who would respond directly to Twitter comments. This theory has helped them be the most effective teleconferencing application presently, particularly during the pandemic period in which most firms turn to work with staff from home situations and students depending on online classes to learn. Basic key performance features are:

- Given a lot in return for a little-HD video conferencing, accessibility, and online meetings all at just $9.99.

- It can run on any platform and any form of a device such as Apple or Microsoft.

- It uses minimal bandwidth to function in a sluggish or poor internet link.

- It has free functionalities such as community video calls.

- 150 milliseconds is all it takes to make sure that conversations over the application are possible.

Customers are truly a major determinant of business performance or collapse. It only took some weeks for Airbnb, which took about ten years to build its brand, to start losing more than half its market value. The coronavirus pandemic is a significant factor in this. Still, it also relies on the company's business orientation being consumer-focused or focused on travelers or short-stay lodgers. When the need changed and request decreased, it had to be halted by the company right in the middle of a planned IPO.

The Unique Selling Proposition (USP) is also a crucial factor in engaging with the main target audiences and the already reached market, including 4Ps, commodities, promo, place, and price. Over time, Zoom modified the topography. It attained its peak during the coronavirus pandemic, especially when digitalization reached the highest level.

Zoom is a perfect instance of a business that found market holes in the teleconferencing industry. Since the company has worked tirelessly for years to establish and market its unique selling proposition (USP), its achievement cannot be due to sheer chance and luck. There may be other rivals in the industry, but with its simplicity and consistency, which other brands struggle to attain, Zoom is unique. Skype may have joined the market first, but Zoom has outperformed them by continually improving their offerings to meet consumer needs and complaints. To not lose grip of its business lead, Zoom must consistently strengthen its USP.

Of note, not all businesses have benefited from the coronavirus pandemic. That was Airbnb's situation, which is going through hard moments due to the travel industry disruptions. Several Airbnb business partners no longer feel secure renting their residences to visitors with no cure to the virus and, rather, capitulate listing their residences on long-term rental businesses. Because of sanitation and health concerns, consumers are often unwilling to remain in Airbnb spaces, leading to a massive reduction in the company's profits and partners.

By obtaining personal input from his former clients, Eric Yuan assessed his intended market. Eric was capable of connecting using the right communication methods. Eric projected his business scale, and he split it into groups by delivering a response to people with similar desires, wishes, and demands, which is an inexpensive and easier online meeting teleconferencing platform.

The consumer has needs/pains, expectations, wishes, and Zoom can address the discomfort, thereby charging a premium for the solution that offers value for customer service, such as warmth rather than wood. Zoom is a phenomenon as it continues to develop, and it knows what people expect, and its customer care technology serves them more than rivals do.

Skype, on the flip side, became weak when it became too stable because it took longer than expected for progress to occur. The peer-to-peer is Skype's strength, and as well as failure, it's fantastic on PCs, but worse on smartphones; it attempted to fix it but takes too much time to move to the cloud. The Microsoft business framework gradually decreased the relevance of the Skype app due to the creation of Microsoft teams that are commonly adopted today, especially for virtual meetings.

Chapter Eleven: Communicate the Idea and its Essence

The secret to creating a profitable organization is superb communication. You must care about giving your clients a clear, strong message. Don't panic if you're a small businessman and are worried that you can't interact well. As with other talents, by practice, you can get stronger through being conscious of this. Below are certain ways experts communicate ideas to their customers and find out why these approaches make sense.

Research Your Audience
It's important that you know your customers if you want to learn how to communicate well. Fortunately, when studying your target group, you do not have to fret about inconsistent assessments anymore. Resources like Facebook Audience Insight enable you to look more closely at the most likely individuals to purchase your service or products. You will find detailed demographic information like lifestyle, relationship status, age, work location, and gender of people involved in what you are providing as it corresponds to Facebook Insight.

Once you have collected data about your customers, you can now go back and concentrate on your selling. To build your email ads, news releases, advertising, and website ad content, leverage what you have heard about prospective clients.

Following findings from Shopify, individuals no longer regard firms as mere producers of goods. They are turning to "lifestyle partners" that the customer returns to time and time again. You ought to connect effectively by approaching and knowing your customers if you wish to create these kinds of connections with them.

Product Launch Presentations

A stage show is one of the easiest ways to interact with your clients or prospective buyers. This is a perfect time to let your ability to interact surface.

A perfect instance of a good stage demonstration emerges from the Bethesda Softworks, a triple-A game studio. They began by creating teaser videos and images on social media leading up to the event. Weeks before the broadcast, their ads began to generate hype about their product launch, and it succeeded!

Everyone was expectant by the time their presentation began. You would like to create that same expectation with your service or product. Bethesda checked through their products, and they made an immense discovery of their tapped commodity at the very end.

You can get the same outcomes! What you have to do is generate excitement leading up to the unveiling of your idea — post-event details, like teasers, on your social media profiles and company websites. Make sure that you talk plainly, with passion, and connect with your viewers as showtime rolls around. You should use a program like Ummo to help you learn whenever you struggle with your "uhh's" and "umm's," until you can talk effectively with little to no stock phrases.

Have a strategy for Social Media
You have to build and execute a stone-solid social media strategy if you want to boost your social media skills. There are two key points you have to do to be able to interact like a professional on social media:
Routinely refresh your Facebook, Twitter, and other social media profiles. Glance through your accounts at some points during the day or at the wake of the morning to see if anyone has commented on your posts. It can be difficult to respond to everyone if you have a lot of followers, but you should try to interact with your customers to the best of your abilities.
To answer the most common questions, you may also set up some regular copy/paste replies. If you want to use this strategy, make sure that you start each answer with the commenter's first name, making the answer sound more intimate. As long as you take the time to get to know your audience, engage on social media, and practice talking to your customers regularly, you will get better!

Chapter Twelve: Manage All Resources

A Temporary Setback

Although Zoom is on an uptrend after its successful IPO in early 2020, the direction that it has been touring has not been totally free of hurdles, illustrated by the quick revolt Zoom witnessed in July 2020 after a bug became apparent in its meeting application. Researchers discovered a security flaw in the software that would have enabled attackers to enter Zoom video conference events on a Mac device that abused public concerns about privacy and cyber security in the technology room.

Although Zoom easily solved the problem with a tiny bug patch, Yuan told CNBC Make It that the event taught him something about how essential it is to easily collect the information as a technology leader and take measures in any scenario featuring a possible security weakness.

According to him, a tech leader must be really practical with some security problems to truly know what the actual issue is and then undertake fast action.

Although Zoom has also witnessed a dramatic rise in the teleconferencing industry and keeps facing intense competition from bigger rivals (such as Microsoft, Google, and Cisco), Eric believes the business still has lots of space to expand. In reality, he assumes that Zoom will someday hit more than one billion user profiles.

Globally, there are more than one billion [office] employees, "he says to CNBC Make It." Our mission is to link the Zoom network to all those one billion information employees. So, considering our current position ... I'd say we were only starting, basically.

The Surge Of Zoom bombing

It was a "wild journey" because it was priced higher than more popular consumer firms such as Pinterest and Lyft, which listed at the same time, the Financial Times noted, on Zoom's successful IPO the year before. Nevertheless, protection and privacy issues are now starting to disrupt its surge: the transformation of Zoom into an also-ran video application, primarily utilized by businesses, has been followed with a spike in the tradition of "zoom bombing"- i.e., gate crashing Zoom meetings. The topic is becoming so widespread that the FBI is now prosecuting, and many class-action cases are confronting Zoom. Yuan continues to apologize and has offered a remedy to the situation. No surprise that Zoom has taken the preventive measures to ensure that the event never takes place again.

Eric apologized to customers for a series of security breaches that have shaken the software recently. Yuan promoted the Zoom's latest privacy changes and vowed to take any flaws strictly, listening to audiences for over two hours.

We Have a Lot of Work to Do

Zoom has also implemented a ninety-day freeze on scheduled features as part of that renewed emphasis, enabling employees to work entirely on tackling issues with their existing offering. The organization unveiled many improvements earlier this week to discourage "zoombombing" and other operation abuse.

Yuan also directly discussed a study released by the Citizen Lab, which found that encrypted data were collected through a China network even though all attendees in the conference were not within the region. According to Eric, the correspondence occurred as a result of client applications trying to contact a scheduling server. Still, he said it occurred in a small number of cases that disappeared. Nevertheless, the very prospect of such contact may unlock the gates to malicious people, rendering the service a serious weakness.

Zoom also facilitates the management of the new privacy and security issues. Alex Stamos, a former Facebook chief security, confirmed that he'd coordinate his intelligence work with Zoom. However, he would not be serving as a Zoom executive or an employee.

US members of Congress and regulators are also scrutinizing Zoom. In a petition to the Federal Trade Commission that Senator Ed Markey sent, he requested for the regulator to provide "comprehensive guidelines for businesses providing teleconferencing solutions and also industry standards for consumers during the coronavirus pandemic and beyond to safeguard online privacy and security." Such regulations will impact not only Zoom but also other rivals like Google Hangouts and Skype.

Chapter Thirteen: Resting Not On Oasis

There is More to be Achieved

Some individuals are fated to be business owners and not work for people for most of their lives. These people are eager to start an enterprise of their own and propel it to greatness from when they got into school, or maybe even before that, and they'll not stop to make that wish come true.

For others, it's a frightening, daunting thought to build a company. So many uncertainties out there to risk the dive. But don't ignore all the advantages associated with having a business if you're contemplating becoming a businessman.

We will give you a myriad of reasons why you should start a company. From something as important as trying to raise some spare cash to more abstract excuses like trying to be the first business to sell hats for birds, we've heard it all. All in all, various persons, for multiple reasons, start their businesses.

There are no justifications, good or bad. Yeah, there are one or two valid excuses why you shouldn't start a company right now. But are they worth it?

Starting a business has shown to be life-changing for so many individuals that it is worth taking into account. Technology is compacting the world, opening up industries, and allowing many individuals to entrepreneur and business owners in an easier way than ever before. Nevertheless, some who sense the pull of passion are terrified to take the plunge. Don't be among those persons who think back and lament never starting a company of their own. Take care of your vision and your destiny. There are numerous strong reasons you need to own a business, and here we have compiled 5 of the most convincing.

Starting a small company is a major risk for someone to take when a more unpredictable financial future may entail sacrificing a normal career's stability and security. Small business progress can also entail a lot of preparation, ample initial funding to help the owner through the start-up phase, and maybe a little luck.

Potential for More Income

When you establish your own company, contingent on your actions and the prosperity or loss of the venture, you can gain an infinite salary. This varies from working for a corporation where your supervisors' payment arrangement or the appraisal of your success may restrict your profits.

Pursuing a Passion

Opening your own company makes it possible for you to make money while pursuing an enterprise that you have a great passion for. You could have a particular skill that you have loved as a sport, such as painting, playing guitar, or fixing cars. You can find more happiness and satisfaction in your work life by

A Good Idea

You may have an insight into a service or product in the industry that fills an unmet need. You would be the first to fill this need by converting your vision into a company, which can lead to a lucrative enterprise. By explaining your concept to others or building a business plan that you would transform into an enterprise, you could benefit even more.

New Lifestyle

Setting up a company can be a method of escaping the corporate sector and enter into a more versatile world for people who are wary of the '9-to-5' routine. Based on the business type that you prefer, you may want a better work-life balance that can enable you to spend quality time with friends and family. Having a company of your own is also ideal if you love making your choices without others' advice.

Self-Expression

Having your own company encourages you to be more innovative and show what you've got to the world. By keeping up with a less fixed work approach, you'll not bet limited, and if you want, you can adjust your process flow in whatever way and direction you want. To satisfy consumer needs, you can even build complementary goods or services.

Chapter Fourteen: Giving Rooms for Improvement

To a business owner, there's nothing more essential to have the right staff. Their ability to deliver will surge if they are motivated, and that's precisely what you'd like to deliver value to customers.

Making subtle improvements to behaviors will dramatically increase the efficiency and workplace effectiveness levels of your company. In a brief span of time, this would enable you to get high-quality work completed and also decrease the number of hours wasted on non-essential works.

Below are eight key takeaways that you can apply to get the best out of the workers to make sure their efficiency is sustained to the maximum:

1. Be Successful

Remember how the organization works at the moment, and be receptive to the opportunity to improve how you work. Know that making long-term and short-term categories are equally as crucial as prioritizing tasks, particularly in a small business.

Is there a simpler way for team members to plan their day in order to encourage them to accomplish their everyday objectives? Create a schedule for each team member and urge all to form a list to make sure that he or she finishes prioritized jobs early and continues on track all day long, leading to successful work completion.

2. Delegate

Having a delegate carries with its risk factor, but enhanced transparency is necessary to boost your workers' productivity and work satisfaction. Offer duties to eligible workers who are successful in a specific area with an established reputation and confidence to handle the assignments well.

If you give workers the ability to learn expertise and leadership skills, your organization will gain from it. It will also give your workers a sense of accomplishment and purpose toward their visions.

3. Minimize disturbances

Social media can hinder productivity, but having a no-phone principle in your establishment is not practical. Alternatively, strive to keep staff concentrated and active while giving them space to breathe.

Motivate staff to switch their mobiles off and observe regular breaks throughout which they can check through their smartphones without interfering with their works. This will guarantee that they discharge their duties better.

4. Have the Right Tools and Equipment

You must provide workers with the correct instruments and tools to discharge their duties efficiently and on schedule. Nothing is more detrimental than wasting hours trying to print documents when you don't have an efficient printer.

High-quality, innovative services and amenities make a big impact on the workers' performance and how the industry is viewed.

5. Improving conditions in the workplace
A workspace that's too cold or too hot draws attention away from the focus, as staff members will spend more time wandering about to get their electric fan or coats. Make sure that as the related season rolls along, all heating and air-conditioning facilities are in good condition.

6. Provide Support and Set Achievable Goals
For administrators, a common cause concern is receiving no straightforward and good understanding of why or not their workers are doing well.
Will the workers need a reason to be on track? Support them by providing attainable targets. Provide managers and workers with specific direction to better articulate objectives. As they will have a strong emphasis and strong priorities, this will serve to improve their effectiveness.

7. Exercise Positive Reinforcement
Motivate, compensate, and inspire. Tell staff they are doing a decent job and give positive reviews when they discharge their duties well. Most notably, give them rewards when you feel they have performed excellently and gone beyond expectations.

To foster a sense of satisfaction to inspire others, you can specifically show one employee's performance to other employees. They are more likely to place higher efficiency on top of their to-do list when you encourage them to work harder and obtain incentives in exchange.

8. Ensure Employees Are Happy

No tangible outcomes can be created in a tense environment. Employees who are continually implored to work in excessively demanding situations are less active and have greater absenteeism and disengagement levels. It's a gratifying but frequently ignored practice of motivating your staff by showing them just how much the company appreciates, supports, and respects them on a human basis. Try out a couple of these strategies and reap the rewards if you want your workers to perform to the best of their abilities.

Chapter Fifteen: Touching the World with the Idea

Zoom Touched the Ends of the Globe

The 9-year-old network has arisen as the desired platform for not only interactive meetings and school lectures, holiday parties, costume celebrations, worship services, picnics, reading groups, and special evenings, as the coronavirus pandemic has compelled millions of people worldwide to remain in their houses. It has also become a central part of online culture, including Twitter and Facebook. The free version of Zoom will accommodate up to 100 people at once.

From the outset, in a market of goods that were undoubtedly more feared than beloved, Zoom strived to stand out. Eric spoke about "how disappointed" consumers were with the teleconference instruments on the teleconference software in a letter to shareholders included in his documentation for making it public a year ago.

The free plan of Zoom will accommodate up to one hundred video attendees at a time. The free Skype edition owned by Microsoft provides only for fifty participants—and includes personable software, such as the capability to select from various backgrounds, alter visual effects, contain secure private calls, send DMs, and capture sessions. The consumer will pay $14.99 annually for unrestricted access if calls go past 40 minutes; enterprise subscription holders can pay only $19.99.

Zoom has debuted as the most popular application on the Apple App Store in previous times, smashing its sales records by more than two times. In accordance with the data analytics company Apptopia, Zoom was downloaded by about 2.13 million times globally, up from 2.04 million the previous day. The software had below 56,000 worldwide downloads some two months before.

However, there are drawbacks to such fast development and the additional expectations that come with it. Zoom now faces questions about anonymity and online abuse, quite like other conventional social media. Already, as idle, quarantined trolls and hackers overtake public video chats by showing graphic material or racist remarks to create a stir, the term "Zoombombing" has arisen. For instance, Chipotle reported to CNN Business that Chiptole Together, a Zoom member, distributed porn to all participants during its latest public teleconference sequence. The organization has changed channels since then. The New York Times first confirmed the matter.

Around the same period, in the midst of growing growth of online networking resources and social channels that have strained even broader channels, including Facebook and its commercial counterpart Instagram, Zoom must strive hard to keep its product running smoothly.

Zoom spokesman Farshad Hashmatulla told CNN that it depends on its network infrastructure in 17 locations worldwide to manage this increase, directing all video and audio data to these sites. He said the Zoom's strategy even before the health scare was to ensure that it could accommodate twice its current daily peak in use and, if appropriate, have the capacity to install tens of thousands of new servers in few hours.

Blood Money: The Argument against using money during the coronavirus pandemic

As the coronavirus pandemic progresses, Zoom now seems to be increasingly extending its role through sectors. For instance, it provides its services to K-12 schools in different countries for no cost. It also exempted its monthly subscription fee in China for all consumers.

Wayne Kurtzman, who studies video conferencing services for market research firm IDC, said, "Zoom knows it will drive their development by many years right now." For the corporation, this is a critical moment by standing forward in a manner that encourages people to be efficient and human.

Zoom is still far from experiencing fast development as the only video messaging tool. Skype for iPhone had more than half a million downloads within one day; WebEx for iPhone, as per Apptopia data, had 89,000 downloads. According to Kurtzman, corporations, including Slack, Microsoft, and Cisco, have also been ready for the moments when an event like this may occur, where they would see exponential growth and sales.

Despite some technological bulges, Microsoft's chat and communications network teams suffered a big blackout in Europe — these main players handled development amazingly well. But it is the potential of Zoom to satisfy the demands of individuals working virtually and to act as a friendly socializing platform.

Ultimately, experts say that new functionalities will need to be added to encourage customers to part with their money. For now, as their virtual workers became relaxed at home and stay focused on ensuring that it works, corporations are mostly wary when introducing new tools.

Chapter Sixteen: Insufficient Funds is never a Threat

Starting a company with low funds calls for a change of mindset. We are typically trained to launch the process of searching for business prospects. The void may be an unfulfilled desire for the consumer or a recent innovation yet to be placed on the market.
Next, we set a target of developing a company that will fill that void. We draft business proposals and submit them with the guarantee of a return on investment to prospective funders.
If the investors like you and like your proposal, they will give you the funds to support the venture.
Many times, individuals find it impossible to collect the funds they need, allowing the whole initiative to crumble on its back. There is an alternate path to establishing a new project.
Examine closely the tools and partnerships that you have control over and analyze how you can easily bring them to use to build a product that the public demands or desires. To assess how the market reacts to multiple offers, you can play with various mixes of resources and create a product that is very attractive to others over time. Using this method, the priorities of an entrepreneur will spring up over time, factoring in the capital, relationships, and contingencies.

They are not resolved at the beginning of a venture as they are when the conventional technique is followed. Using the metaphor of the dinner party is a helpful way to distinguish the conventional and alternative ways of venture development. Assume that on a Sunday night, you are meeting a few mates for a relaxed sit-down meal. You could take time to think about who is arriving and what food they want in preparation for this social gathering.

How to Raise Money for Your Business through Your IPO

For fundraising, most financiers favor an IPO as it provides the best valuation in most situations. When a purchase is not feasible, a business doing a repurchase will almost always go through the IPO method. Yet somehow, the corporation organizes a re-funding in which the shares held by the initial owners is repurchased.

IPOs are obviously elegant and generally yield their Initial public offering investors the highest returns, but, for a multitude of reasons, they are not often sufficient for the business owners and the executive team in the longer term.

Benefits of Obtaining Capital from IPO

- **Financing**

The main motivation for an IPO is to collect a large sum of cash that does not have to be remitted. Hence the business does not need to part with preexisting capital to acquire ownership of the company.

- **Follow-On Financing**

By selling new shares in a public offering, a listed corporation will collect more money, and so there can now be a contingency source to raise money for the good of the company.

- **Understanding Preceding Investments**

Whenever a business goes public, customers know the worth of their contribution before the IPO. What's more, once the lock-up phase comes to an end, their stock is available and can be traded on the stock exchange. Previous investments will, however, be gotten now.

- **Visibility and Reputation**

A public corporation gets greater credibility and is more recognizable. Sometimes this helps the business to advertise and distribute its goods outsource, staff recruiting, and financing.

- **Employees' Benefits**

Stock options already owned by or issued to workers in the future have a known benefit and thus provide a favorable opportunity to pay the workers.

- **Acquiring other companies**

A company that went public can utilize its shares to purchase other businesses, and it is also a reasonable option to purchase smaller or related businesses in order to extend the customer base or acquire a new customer base.

Downsides of Acquiring Capital from Initial Public Offerings

- **Higher Costs**

The accrued expenditures related to going public are quite high. These comprise of accounting and legal payments, postage charges, and licensing fees. If the business does not eventually go public, these costs are not salvageable, which occurs to almost half the businesses that start on the IPO process and were not able to have it completed. When the business goes public, about seven percent of the money earned is taken by the insurer.

- **Public Fishbowl**

SEBI guidelines mandate that when a business goes public, it should reveal a large amount of knowledge about itself, which was confidential and accessible only to stakeholders until then. That data covers officer and manager salaries, executive equity option plans, large arrangements such as rental and advisory deals, specifics of activities, including corporate strategy, revenue, sales expenses, gross revenues, net earnings, debt, and plans for the future. The prospectus for the Initial public offering and other papers that may be sent to the SEBI is in the public's domain.

- **Short-Term Time Horizon**

Investors and market advisers anticipate ever-growing success quarter by quarter after an Initial public offering. This presumption forces the company's leadership to concentrate on optimizing short-term gains instead of pursuing long-term targets. This will damage the profitability of business earnings in the long term.

- **Management's Time**

After an Initial public offering, the Executive and the chief financial officer have to spend quality time with investment experts, institutional investors, financial journalists, and other shareholders because they build a market for the company's stock. This is a diversion from their primary task, which is running the business for optimum production. Some major businesses have managers whose primary task is to handle investor relations.

- **Takeover Goal**

Often, a public corporation becomes the victim of another businesses' unexpected acquisition. This is regarded as an unfriendly acquisition that can cause all sorts of problems for the organization.

- **Employee Disenchantment**

As the price of the stocks rises, it equally surges workers' courage, but it can be demotivating when it sinks, particularly when the options of a worker go "underwater". Underwater factors can make motivating and retaining key staff challenging.

When a businessman gets donations from an investor such as a venture capitalist or a business angel, a future harvest should be in place when the harvest is realizable. The harvest is originally for consumers instead of businessmen.

Chapter Seventeen: Strategies to be Above Board

How to Guarantee That Your Business Is Running Above Board

You'll frequently have heaps of ideas and visions of your intended business and the objectives you want to accomplish as you go into business. Bu then, it can be a frightening and thrilling experience often so that you might also be a bit inexperienced. And you're still going to be a bit inexperienced compared to having exposure and operating your own business for years. But it can take you the unintended route sometimes.

When it has to do with bad business handling, this is certainly the case. It is essential to note the destruction of industries by shady dealings so that you can have no hand in it. Perhaps, not even understanding how to get there, you may catch yourself on a dangerous path. So these suggestions can come in handy if you want to make sure that the business runs above board all the time.

Be Straightforward Financially

The first method to guarantee that you are on the correct the right path is to keep your finances open so that no doubt can be entertained. Although you do not wish to reveal the complete details of your financial affairs to the whole world, you should appear as truthful and straightforward as practicable. This ensures that you would choose to partner with a good and fair corporate finance firm to make sure that you adopt the best policies, remit your taxes, and run as a responsible corporation in general.

Employ the People that you can Vouch For
From here, integrating yourself with the right staff is going to be the next task. It's essential that you employ people that you can vouch for. You should still know what the workers are doing and be able to believe that they are not poorly operating the business.

Root Ethically
Your bad decisions can also be as easy as collaborating with the wrong vendors. Consumers do not only think about responsible sourcing practices but also think about serving humanity. This implies not causing harm and playing fair. So one homework you want to do is to do your research well and pick your suppliers.

Let Your Competition be Fair
One step you want to make sure that you do not trivialize is how you treat your rivals. This is because you can get it wrong if you don't apply the right methods, and you can also get it right if you do it well. You may have the suspicion not to engage in anticompetitive practices, but it is in your best interest to steer clear from this. It may do your business harm. Engaging in a competition is your best bet, and do so honorably while also hoping to win.

Do Not Yield

Above all else, you need to stand your ground when it comes to what you believe in. Because you may find that, at some point during your tenure as head of your business, you feel pressure to do things that are not quite above board. Whether it's the devil on your shoulder telling you it's the easiest solution or others in the industry. But you need to stay strong and ensure that you do business your way, and you'll always do well.

In all you do, make sure that you stand firm in what you believe in and do not yield; else you may witness all you've labored crumbling before you.

Chapter Eighteen: Your Family Matters

Family is More Important

Nothing beats family. No endeavor is more important than frequently connecting with your family and showing them that you care. Being an entrepreneur has not made this any easier. Warren Buffets us it better when he admonished us not to trivialize the important things at the expense of things that are not important to us. One of the best things you can ever do for yourself as an entrepreneur is to strike a balance between the amount of time you devote to your family and your work life.

Keeping Your Family Happy As a Businessman/Entrepreneur

- **Make them Your Priority**

Captains of industry like Eric Yuan and other billionaires are known to be family people. Family is a source of strength, and the immense encouragement they can give us can be the primary motivator we need to succeed. It is not enough that you only think about it. It is important that you set and achieve family goals. For instance, how often do you reach out to them? When was the last time you told them something endearing? While most people will readily leave you to bear your cross in the event of a mishap, your family members are some of the people you can bank on to help you back on your feet. If you ignore this idea of making your family members your priority, the repercussions may be more than what you bargained for.

According to Brock Blake, an entrepreneur, three of the top priorities that he never misses are; a weekly date with his sweetheart wife, moments he spends with his children, and family dinner.

One thing is very important to take into account. Irrespective of how crucial it is to succeed in your business, family is not meant to be joked with. If not for anything, it is for the fact that they are there with you all through your years spent on earth. Hence, a best practice is to schedule your activities in such a way that periods with them are also factored in.

Make Your Plans and Do it Intelligently.

You've immediately had your priorities clear cut; use the same energy to draft out the step-by-step process that you want to apply to achieve them. Whatever plan you have drafted out, ensure that you factor in family time, work time, mealtime, and the time you dedicate for some special events. Even though it may appear unproductive to make out times for these seeming unprofessional moments, the truth is that they are a great energizer for you. Sheryl Sandberg, Facebook's COO, said that she ensure that she goes to work around 5:30 pm every day. Her top priority to make out time for her family, and it is part of her calculation to make sure she leaves home early to make this feasible.

Organize Yourself
In the end, it might be easier to make a plan than to remain true to it in reality. One or the other will still be competing for your attention and driving the rest of the priority stuff backward.

Applications for appointments and sessions, a new challenge, a new rival, or other forthcoming deadlines can be made. To make exceptions to the schedule, they will become excuses. Your goals will really be checked through these periods, and it will be up to you to manage these things without modifying the schedule.

Sacrifice and Hard Work

You should put in more work and make some compromises to keep being coordinated. Execute your agenda and adhere to your goals. Social interactions with friends or acquaintances may need to be temporarily forgone, but not altogether neglected. Additionally, it might be appropriate to add some late night or early mornings to your work period. Without interruption, these continuous work cycles would enable you to catch up with tasks and emails.

Work Smarter, not Tougher
Everyone is still too busy in today's corporate world trying to get something done, and this is taken as a matter of pride. Being busy is seen as a symbol of success. However, effective business owners develop programs that encourage them to spend time with their family, enjoy weekends and, when they can, and take vacations. These individuals have learned to prioritize and prepare as well as assign tasks to competent persons. A smart way to do this is to analyze your time to see if you spend time on things that are no relevant. Identify whether the activities you are interested in, and you're your assessment to know if they bring value for the organization. Identify which roles may also be transferred to others without a lack of performance or direction.

Be Thankful
By remembering their sacrifice and insight into your life, one great idea of keeping your family happy. Take a moment, every day, to give thanks. It should be a spontaneous act. It will impress close relatives as you mention it when they least expect. Constantly practicing joy will help sustain a state of happiness.

Know When to Say No
The businessman or Chief executive is always the most active and often considered the company's most significant entity. This is the thought pattern of the businessman himself and others close that are close to him. However, you will need to concentrate on your family and your well-being and increase the business. This is why saying no and refocusing on your goals is crucial. You would be able to move on to activities that do not completely need your attention with sufficient assignment to your team's right individuals. Growing a business is not a short race, but a long one, and for long-term sustainability, you need to hold your family relationships together.

Promote Harmony
It is crucial to describe what a peaceable day would appear for you and your family while preparing your schedule. This may include carrying children before going to work to kindergarten, going home for dinner, or finishing your work earlier. Harmony would also mean encouraging yourself to wander a little from your planned work plan and your strategy. This helps to create time for emergencies or family gatherings, or anything else you need.

Communicating Information And Sharing It

Interaction is another path to growth for entrepreneurs. This goes above instruments and dates and is more fundamental than that. Spend some time communicating with your partner and children every day to figure out what has happened in the family and where assistance is needed. Furthermore, don't conceal it when there is a difficult situation at home or at work.

Observe Family Holidays

Holidays seem to indicate lots of money, but a holiday together with your family can ultimately towards a big step to improving the relationship of a family and making everyone pleased. A well-planned holiday will not disrupt your company, but rather both sides will feel the impact.

Chapter Nineteen: Go Legal

Build the Legal Bridges of Your Business

Young entrepreneurs strive to turn their ambitions into a company every new year. These companies often spill with enormous concepts, energy, and positivity, but they do not always have a framework for the legalities associated with starting a company. It's all too simple to put off some of the less stylish, more organizational parts of operating a business in the deluge of gaining new clients, preparing for your site launch, and developing the first design.

Yes, the most thrilling components of your new business are not company regulations and fillings. Yet they are crucial to the quality of your company and your finances. Below is a brief summary of eight different organizational aspects that you have to consider adopting in your small business or start-up. For sure, and contingent on the condition you find yourself in and the business type you operate, employing a financial adviser or a lawyer with a certain experience in your sector will really help you stay away from negative eventualities.

1. Have You Chose a Brand Name? Ensure that You are Legally Backed to Use the Name

Even before you think of having your business card printed, ensure that the brand name that you are settling for is not taken by someone else already. In most instances, you don't need a lawyer's services to carry out this task because you can make use of the power of the internet to investigate if the name has been taken. As the repository for the Secretary of State, several resources are a great place to know if you can set up your kind of business in a particular state. After then, you can run a trademark search to know if the name is available for use.

2. Register a False Business DBA/Name

Has it ever come to your knowledge about the false name publications in the classified of your newspaper? If you intend to start a business, you may need one of these names for your business. If your company might do business using another designation, you may need to file for the Doing Business As form (DBA form). This form is also important if you have a general partnership or a sole proprietorship, as it will help you carry out your business with another name different from the name you registered with.

3. Form an LLC or Have Your Business Incorporated

Forming an incorporation or an LLC is a crucial process needed to safeguard your assets (like the college fund of your child or your personal property) from any liabilities of your company. There are disadvantages and advantages of each business framework, contingent on your defined circumstances. Three of the most common ones are the S corporation (perfect for qualified small business owners), the LLC (ideal for small business that is seeking some legal backing, but without much sophistication), or the C corporation (for companies that want to go public or seeking funding from a VC).

4. Obtain a Tax ID Number from the Federal Government

You will need to acquire a Federal Tax Identification Number, also regarded as an Employer Identification Number (EIN), to differentiate your business as a distinct business entity. The tax ID number is assigned by the IRS and is comparable to your private social security number and enables the IRS to monitor the money transfers of your business. You are not required to obtain a tax ID number if you are a sole owner, but it is still advisable to not offer your private social security number for business dealings.

5. Learn About Laws for Employees

As fast as you hire your first worker, your contractual requirements as an employer also start. To truly comprehend your responsibilities for these processes, try spending time with an employment law expert: state and federal payroll and withdrawing taxes, self-employment taxes, anti-discrimination legislation, OSHA guidelines, unemployment benefits, employee compensation guidelines, and hour and wage demands.

6. Get the Vital Business Licenses and Permits

You may be expected to get one or more business permits or licenses from the local, state, or even national level, contingent on the company form and geographical area. These licenses entail a generic license for commercial activities, licenses for planning and land use, a sales tax permit, licenses for the health sector, and professional or technical licenses.

7. File for Trademark Protection

You're not allowed by the legislation to file a trademark without formal identification. However, Trademark law is difficult, as anticipated, and merely filing a DBA in your state does not grant you common-law privileges immediately. The name needs to be 'trademarkable' and in use in commerce to claim the initial position.

Think about filing your trademark for appropriate legal defense because you have spent countless hours thinking up the perfect brand, and you can put still more work into building brand recognition. Registering a trademark makes retrieving your rights exponentially faster, such as if someone happens to use your business name as a Twitter address. Getting the proper paperwork ensures that you have the legitimate right to do so, and Twitter will take action to supply you with it.

8. Create an Account and begin building business credit

Your mortgage, auto loan, and personal credit cards all determine your eligibility to apply for a business loan because you depend on your credit to finance your enterprise. Your transactions are segregated from those of the organization by the use of corporate credit. You should create an account in your brand's name to start building your business credit, and it should display a cash balance worthy of receiving a bank loan.

Place Your statutory Ducks in a Row.

Allocate a period to resolve these problems and carefully take your legal responsibilities, irrespective of your start-up's schedules. Getting your legal ducks in a row right from the start will help you avoid any pitfalls down the road and will help you scale your business successfully as you grow.

Chapter Twenty: Sustainability: A Must

Eric's Formula for Sustainability

More than just building a business, securing it, making sure that its scale is your utmost priority. If you do not set up structures to secure and sustain your business idea, you may risk what you've built over the years crumbling before you. The business world is filled with stories of entrepreneurs who went out to build a business and have their business crashed back on them because they were not predictive enough to see what the immediate future holds. You sure don't want the same thing to happen to you.

The case is quite different at Zoom. Zoom was lucky to have a CEO like Eric. Eric Yuan has done his assignment to ensure that Zoom is always in line with the industry's demands. This ability to see what the future holds is better accurately shown when Eric foresaw the advantages of a portable teleconferencing application in the coming years. Other teleconferencing app makers were busy innovating their application to do something else. At the same time, Eric rode on the smartphone revolution's wings in the telecommunication industry to make an application that sells. If you want to champion an enterprise that scales, the steps below will guide how exactly how you should go about it.

Six Important Steps That Can Help You Sustain Your Business Idea

1. Test Your Business Idea on Consumers Who Can Afford it

Just because you think an idea is brilliant does not imply that it'll scale. To measure a true need from people who can pay it for it, who don't have a more feasible option out there now, use social networking sites, blogs, crowd financing, or recorded study.

2. To measure costs, build a realistic market operational framework.

Some visions sound amazing, but they might not be feasible or tested with today's technologies yet. Others can be so thrilling that you'll see many rivals competing for the same room. Taking notes of key criteria will allow you to consolidate the information and stick to them mentally.

3. Make sure the idea is reasonable and relevant to your industry.

Unfortunately, since most aspiring entrepreneurs don't have the intellectual property or resources to contend with the copycats or major companies who see the opportunity as fast as they enter the markets, they are often doomed to fail. Today, any start-up without trade secrets, patents, or any other confidential sauce is very risky. Just a tentative patent is enough to retain your position over a year, can be achieved at a low price by your team, and will at least allow major rivals to purchase your idea instead of stealing it. Until you have a tenable alternative to sell, most buyers may not consider you.

4. Plan your promotional story for investors and customers.

A novel idea cannot be so intuitive that it would deliver on its own. Start by making an "elevator pitch," which you will execute to impress a new client or partner in less than a minute. Present at industry events and link to build your audience with your pitch.

5. Let the service or product come to life.

Even before launching your product or service, all the arrangements should deliver your solution and help it. This involves hiring and legitimately presenting the firm as a corporation or an LLC, establishing a business licensing and website, and planning for development, service, and distribution.

6. Adopt a development and enhancement plan.

There is a need for a vision and roadmap for constant growth, innovative products, and an increasing consumer base for an organization to be competitive in this age of accelerated change. This is the stage you have to handle metrics, work on your business ethos, and search for growth dependent on collaborators. Now you can see that, from your idea alone, you, as well as investors and advisors, cannot estimate a market success. In reality, the consistent theme in all these steps is "you." Due to this, professional investors will tell you they do not invest in the horse but rather in the jockey. Without execution, a good plan and thinking about a brilliant solution won't make a successful company.

Chapter Twenty-One: Project for the Future

Do Not Neglect the Future

Nobody will define the modern world as an easy one. It's complicated. There is a fresh and challenging facing most organizations per second. People are continually flooded with commercial advertisements that have turned them pessimistic, not to add that they have little time to devote to other people. There is a growing world of choices for customers and new methods to access them. There are petabytes of data and information at their disposal and different networks where they can explore things that catch their fancy.

In this present environment, the growing pace at which we all function illustrates why such an ancient term-relevance- is unexpectedly essential.

Literally, and particularly socially, companies that serve enough importance to their customer base are relevant. Most people put their attention almost exclusively on something realistic, and that's reasonable. It is correct that what product or service you sell must meet a customer's desires if your business must perform well.

Three Strategies for Relevance

What are the strategies to employ to keep being relevant in your industry? The three strategies below will show you how.

1. Segment Your Promotions

You can't be everything to everyone. The rule is that there are different reasons why you will be important to different people. By separating the ads by very particular aspects such as income, age, gender, schooling, geography, life experience, desires, politics, etc., you will figure out which component would connect with your marketing. Then decide how you can position your business to make it important to such people.

2. Understand Immaterial Triggers

Four key elements will influence customers' perceptions of your service or product, although mostly on a threshold they can't comprehend: values, community, sensory appeal, and thinking. Identify these triggers and taking advantage of them.

3. Take the Three Cs into Account

Significance relies on three circumstances – contact, context, and content. Being in contact with them is one of the ways you can remain relevant to your customer base. Context, which implies space and time, is one other key factor. Content is the third factor; relevance depends on the quality of the content you are dishing out to your customers. Substandard content will attract diminishing significance and vice versa.

www.ingramcontent.com/pod-product-compliance
Lightning Source LLC
Chambersburg PA
CBHW070443220526
45466CB00004B/1761